· Q SERIES

Macbeth

Lance Hattatt and James Sale

HODDER AND STOUGHTON
LONDON   SYDNEY   AUCKLAND   TORONTO

Acknowledgments

The authors and publishers would like to thank the following for permission to reproduce copyright texts: Paul Engle for his poem 'Sonnet 72' from *American Child* by Paul Engle; George Allen & Unwin for an extract from *Fellowship of the Ring* by J. R. R. Tolkien; Bantam Books for an extract from *The Farthest Shore* by Ursula le Guin; the Royal Shakespeare Company for quotations by Judi Dench and Trevor Nunn which appeared in the *Royal Shakespeare Company Broadsheet – Macbeth*, 1981; Arrow Publications for an extract from *No Turn Unstoned* by Diana Rigg; Times Newspapers Ltd for a review by Peter Kemp *Times Literary Supplement* (18.11.83).

The photos in this volume are reproduced by kind permission of the following: the Victoria and Albert Museum (p. 35); Chichester Festival Theatre (p. 36); Joe Cocks Studio (p. 37 top left and p. 41); Dominic Photography (p. 37 top right, bottom left); Royal Shakespeare Company (p. 37 bottom right); the National Gallery (p. 40 left); and the Tate Gallery (p. 40 right).

ISBN 0 340 39297 5

First published 1987

Copyright © 1987 Lance Hattatt & James Sale

All rights reserved. No part of this publication may be reproduced or transmitted in any form or by any means, electronic or mechanical, including photocopy, recording, or any information storage and retrieval system, without permission in writing from the publisher or under licence from the Copyright Licensing Agency Limited. Further details of such licences (for reprographic reproduction) may be obtained from the Copyright Licensing Agency Limited, of 7 Ridgmount Street, London WC1E 7AE.

Photoset by Rowland Phototypesetting Limited,
Bury St Edmunds, Suffolk
Printed in Great Britain
for Hodder and Stoughton Educational
a division of Hodder and Stoughton Limited, Mill Road,
Dunton Green, Sevenoaks, Kent by
St Edmundsbury Press Limited, Bury St Edmunds, Suffolk

Preface

Q is a series of English/Drama booklets for use with mixed-ability groups in the middle years of the secondary school. Standing independently of the text to which it relates, each booklet explores a well-known play through an informal but developing pattern of plot, character, theme, language and theatre.

Each section invites 'dipping-in'. Pupils will discover a wide range of lively and stimulating activities. These vary from discussion to writing, from recording to acting, and are designed to provide insight into a number of relevant and interesting topics.

Dark Deeds

Your teacher will have told you Shakespeare's **The Tragedie of Macbeth**. But what is a 'Tragedie' (or Tragedy, as it is now spelt)?

Is this a tragedy?
No, an accident.

Is this a tragedy?
No, an act of sabotage.

Is this a tragedy?
No, an act of war.

Strictly speaking, none of these events is a tragedy, yet most people today would call them so. What they mean by tragedy is an unnecessary waste and loss of human life. But Shakespeare would not have agreed.

Shakespeare had some definite ideas about tragedy. Some of his ideas are difficult but the main ones – and therefore the most important – are really very easy to understand.

Shakespeare's Tragedy
1 Mainly concerns the fortunes of one person: the hero.
2 The hero has a great weakness of character.
3 The weakness of character causes events of anguish, suffering and misfortune.
4 These events horrify and fascinate the audience.
5 They also lead to the hero's death.

So, if we look at **The Tragedy of Macbeth**, where are these five points to be found?

Macbeth's Tragedy
1 This is shown by the prophecy of the witches and
   Macbeth's response. (I.iii)
2 'Thou wouldst be great,
   Art not without **ambition**, . . .' (I.v)
3 '. . . the affliction of these terrible dreams
   That shakes us nightly;' (III.ii)
4 Witches, treason, murder, ghosts, battle . . .
   Are these ordinary?
5 'Behold where stands
   The usurper's cursed head.' (V.vi)

You will have discovered by now that you need to look at the play. To make the events of **Macbeth** easier for you to understand, we have prepared a story chart. Follow this and find out for yourself what happens. The references direct you to the scenes of greatest interest.

Before looking at them, it will be useful to practise using play references.

PLAYS   are divided into ACTS
ACTS   are divided into SCENES
SCENES   are composed of LINES spoken by characters

Acts are big divisions in the story. In **Macbeth**:
Act 1 – plans against King Duncan   (I.)
Act 2 – action against King Duncan   (II.)
Act 3 – reign of King Macbeth   (III.)
Act 4 – plans against King Macbeth   (IV.)
Act 5 – actions against King Macbeth   (V.)

Scenes break the Act down into smaller pieces, or the particular incidents that make up the Act. So, in Act III, the reign of Macbeth, Macbeth does several things:

he plots Banquo's murder	(III.i)
he explains his worries to his wife	(III.ii)
the murder of Banquo occurs	(III.iii)
Macbeth holds a banquet	(III.iv)
witches prepare to meet Macbeth	(III.v)
the nobles express dissatisfaction with Macbeth	(III.vi)

Lastly, the lines characters speak are simply numbered in order. Turn to Act 2, scene 3, line 26 (written as II.iii.26) and we find:

MACDUFF: What three things does drink especially provoke?

II.iii.27 is the next line:

PORTER: Marry, Sir, nose-painting, sleep, and urine.

Now practise finding references:
- III.iv.35
- IV.i.110
- IV.iii.85
- V.i.20
- V.ix.40
- I.iii.26
- I.v.37
- II.iii.62

The story chart gives us a picture of the whole play, whereas really **Macbeth** is not **one** action, or **one** incident, but a series of smaller events and happenings. Each one may be seen as a building block which fits together to form the whole construction. Any of the 'bricks' which make up the play can be examined in detail. We have taken 'Duncan's Murder' and have shown it in two different news stories.

In the **Glamis Gazette** the murder is reported in a very factual and unsensational way, whereas in the **Scottish Star** less information is given but the writing appeals to you directly and is much easier to read.

Which do you prefer? What advantages does each paper have?

PLOT

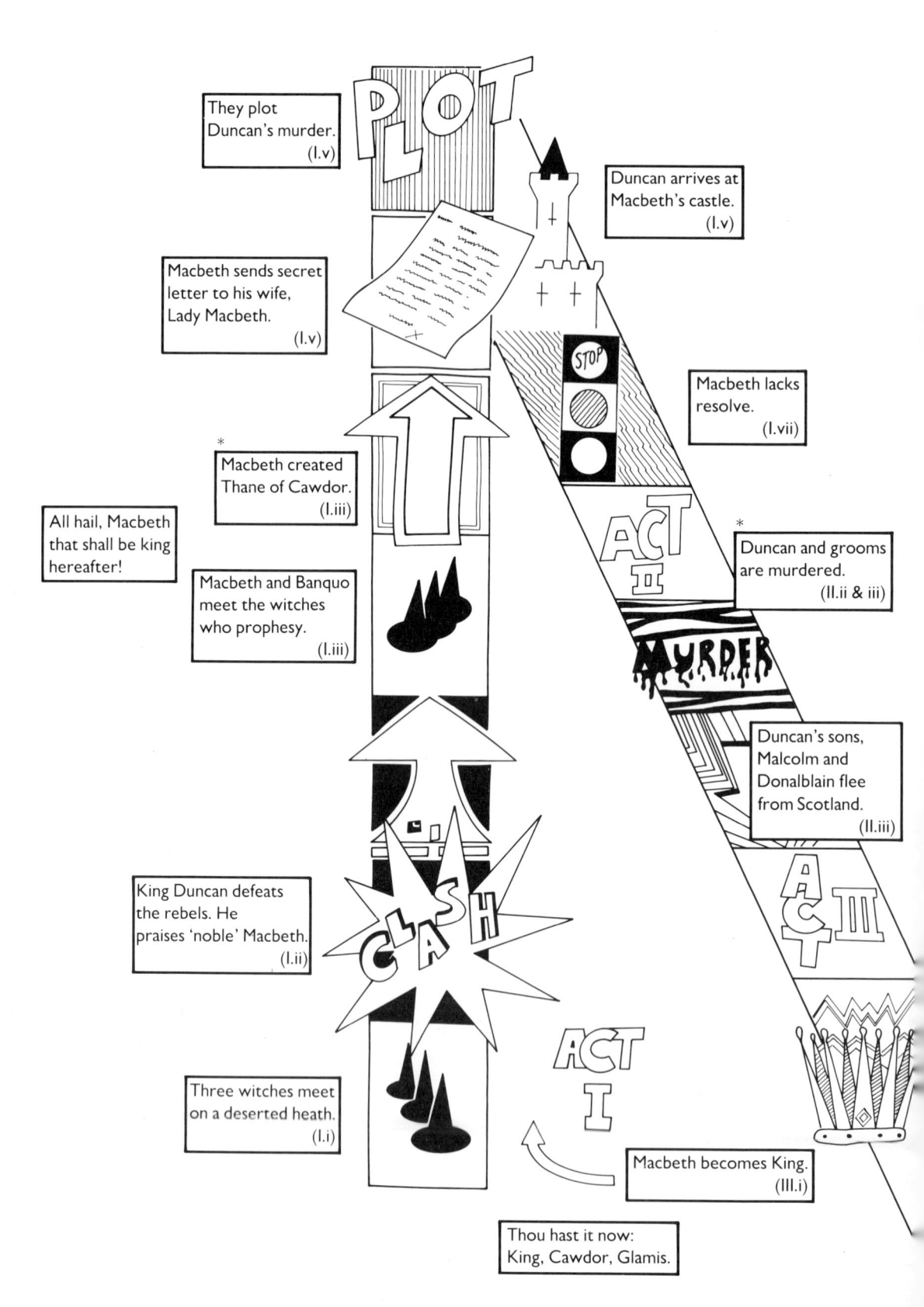

They plot Duncan's murder. (I.v)

Duncan arrives at Macbeth's castle. (I.v)

Macbeth sends secret letter to his wife, Lady Macbeth. (I.v)

Macbeth lacks resolve. (I.vii)

*Macbeth created Thane of Cawdor. (I.iii)

ACT II

*Duncan and grooms are murdered. (II.ii & iii)

All hail, Macbeth that shall be king hereafter!

Macbeth and Banquo meet the witches who prophesy. (I.iii)

MURDER

Duncan's sons, Malcolm and Donalblain flee from Scotland. (II.iii)

ACT III

King Duncan defeats the rebels. He praises 'noble' Macbeth. (I.ii)

CLASH

ACT I

Three witches meet on a deserted heath. (I.i)

Macbeth becomes King. (III.i)

Thou hast it now: King, Cawdor, Glamis.

8

Uprising planned against Macbeth.
(IV.iii)

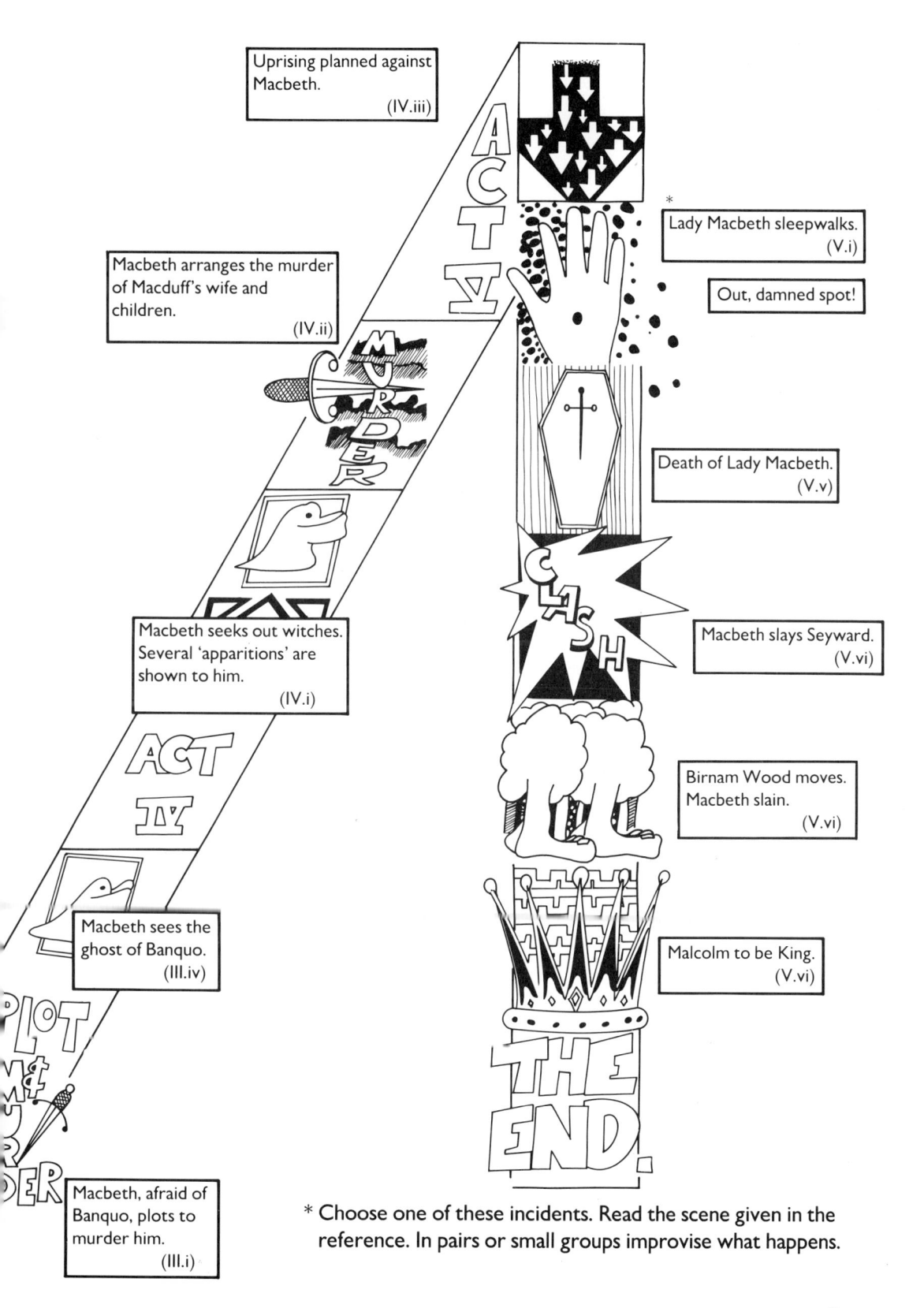

Lady Macbeth sleepwalks.
(V.i) *

Out, damned spot!

Macbeth arranges the murder of Macduff's wife and children.
(IV.ii)

Death of Lady Macbeth.
(V.v)

Macbeth slays Seyward.
(V.vi)

Macbeth seeks out witches. Several 'apparitions' are shown to him.
(IV.i)

Birnam Wood moves. Macbeth slain.
(V.vi)

ACT IV

Malcolm to be King.
(V.vi)

Macbeth sees the ghost of Banquo.
(III.iv)

THE END.

Macbeth, afraid of Banquo, plots to murder him.
(III.i)

* Choose one of these incidents. Read the scene given in the reference. In pairs or small groups improvise what happens.

SMOCK GATHERING EASY TO USE!
NO FUSS!
only £1.00 plus £5.00 carriage
WARWICK WOOD
STRATFORD ON AVON
WARWICKSHIRE

THE GLAMIS GAZETTE

16 NOVEMBER 1632   NO. 1450751   PRICE 3d

WELL! WELL! WELL!
The REAL Wishing Well
£2 inc P&P
WITCHES CAVERN
HAYWARDS HEATH SUSSEX

SLEEP NO MORE KING MURDERED!

Murder and Treason

Fear and terror struck the hearts of all innocent men last night when, after hours of wild speculation and rumour, the murder of the King, Duncan, was finally confirmed.

The King, in order to honour the Thane of Glamis, Macbeth, to whom he had recently given the title of Cawdor, was at the castle to celebrate victory over the rebels in the recent battles. Upon instruction Macduff, a trusted and respected Thane, entered the Royal apartments at an early hour to be confronted by the sight of an open door and the disgorged body of the King, his silver skin laced with golden blood.

To the shouts of murder and treason the alarm was raised and the household quickly assembled. Macbeth, displaying great emotion, told of how, upon learning of the King's murder, he had gone straight to the scene of the crime and killed the two guards believing them to have been responsible for the dreadful deed. The guards he called murderers, 'steeped in the colours of their trade, their daggers unmannerly breached with gore'.

Lady Macbeth, overcome, apparently fainted and had to be carried off.

Sons Suspected

Doubts have already been cast about possible motives the guards could have for this bloody murder. Suspicion is rapidly fastening on the two princes, Malcolm and Donalblain, who have already fled the country. Meanwhile rumours continue to circulate that Macbeth is to succeed to the throne.

Exclusive Interview

In an exclusive interview with the **Glamis Gazette**, Ross, a Thane of Scotland, told of various premonitions that occurred during the night of the murder. The strangest of these was his report of Duncan's horses, the finest thoroughbreds in the land, which, he said, turned wild, broke from their stalls and eventually devoured each other. Clearly these are dangerous and uncertain times. But naturally our readers will be kept informed of further developments as they occur.

STOP PRESS — Malcolm sighted in England. Border alert.

SCOTTISH STAR

NO. 371996
PRICE......ONE GROAT

WIN YOURSELF A WEEDRAM P.6

P.8 PLAY BAGPIPE BINGO

MURDER
WITCH REVEALS ALL!

Duncan is dead! Murder most foul! The nation mourns but demands justice.

Early this morning the Thane of Fife – twenty-third in line to the throne – entered the Royal bedchamber and found his master and dear overlord brutally assassinated by his very own guards.

Macbeth, the King's cousin, accompanied by his young wife wearing a pink negligé, slaughtered the butchers in a fit of rage.

Two mysteries remain! Who hired the butchers to do their atrocity? How did the witches know this was going to happen?

Interviewed by our man on the spot, Jimmy Stewart, Hecate, leader of the coven, said, 'It was in the stars and now the cauldron sings'.

Meanwhile Scotland mourns the passing of a great and noble king. Who will succeed?

Although newspapers did not exist in Shakespeare's time, these stories of one event in the play appear as they might have done in the press.

A number of other incidents could easily make newsworthy stories. Which kind of treatment would you give them?

1 The Battle of Forres (I.ii) with the confrontation between 'the merciless Macdonwald' and 'brave Macbeth'.
2 An eye-witness account of the execution of the Thane of Cawdor (I.iii).
3 The discovery of Macbeth's letter to Lady Macbeth (I.v) with comment on its political implications.
4 The reception of Duncan at Macbeth's castle near Inverness (I.vi).
5 The murder of Banquo and the escape of Fleance (III.iii).
6 'Birnam Wood Removes to Dunsinane'. Use this as your headline to lead the story of the final battle (V.iii).

You are now in the fortunate position of having been invited to **two** coronations: Macbeth's (II.iv) and Malcolm's (V.vi). But oh, how different each is.

> The Lord High Chamberlain
> Commands
>
> To Attend
> The Coronation of

The coronation of Macbeth occurs in circumstances of suspicion, hostility and intrigue where the atmosphere is charged with gloom and foreboding.

The coronation of Malcolm, in contrast, is joyous, open and acclaimed, an occasion of splendour and majesty, because the new king has freed the people from the tyranny of Macbeth.

You are commanded to write an account of both of these coronations for inclusion in a new history book, **Out of the Dark Years**, which Malcolm is to have distributed to all Scottish schools.

You can, of course, include your own drawings, diagrams, illustrations and pictures of such diverse features of the coronation as banners, uniforms, costumes, regalia, heraldry, weaponry, architecture, scenery and behaviour.

Instead of writing about the coronations, you may like to make up and act out a play about either one.

In exile our historian discovers that Malcolm has maintained a secret correspondence with his brother, Donalblain. These letters concern the political situation in Scotland during the reign of Macbeth.

Imagine you are one of the princes. Write a letter to your brother. These are suggestions for things to include in your letter:

>   The murder of Banquo. (III.iii)
>   Macbeth's banquet and its abrupt ending. (III.iv)
>   Macbeth using the supernatural. (IV.i)
>   The slaughter of Lady Macduff and her children. (IV.ii)
>   The flight of Macduff. (IV.iii)
>   The testing of Macduff. (IV.iii)
>   The planned invasion. (IV.iii)

'Macbeth slain', so say the stage directions (V.vi). But is this the end? For Macbeth, yes, but . . .

. . . what now? Is this 'happy ever after' for Malcolm, the new King of Scotland? Has evil finally perished from the land? What ever happened to the witches? Will Donalblain be content as **only** brother to the King? Will Fleance succeed to the throne?

None of these questions has a real answer in Shakespeare's **Macbeth**. However, it can be fun to imagine. Imagine that you are writing Act VI in which some of these questions can be answered. Before beginning, you should re-examine the last scene of Act V and take special note of the way the play is set out. Of course, you do not have to write your speeches as Shakespeare's poetry, but do try to show clearly the characters you present.

Having written Act VI, tape it. Include music and sound effects where appropriate.

Murderer to Monarch

There is no doubt; the Macbeth story is very exciting.

Turn to the list of characters (sometimes called the 'Dramatis Personae') at the beginning of the play. Most characters have names, but those without are still important.

1 Choose one character, say who you are. Form a line that reflects your rank in society at the start of the play. First will come King Duncan. But who is second? Where would a witch fit in? Disagreements of positioning should be discussed.

2 What would the line be like at the beginning of III.i? At this point Duncan is dead (whoever plays his role can choose another).

3 Allow the characters in the play to meet each other – it's a party! Just mingle, introduce yourself to someone else, discuss who you are and who they are.
Try to think through your character: the gentlewoman's name, for example, might be Maria; she comes from Edinburgh and has been with Lady Macbeth for 2 years; she's not entirely happy living at Glamis Castle . . . Lady Macbeth is . . . and, well . . . she cannot say too much, but . . .
Talk freely to each other.

4 After 10 or 15 minutes a signal indicates the party is over. The room is now the Throne room in the palace/castle.
Position yourselves.
Where is the king? Does he sit or stand? How do you indicate that he is above everyone else?
Use chairs and rostra blocks – you should find these helpful.

5 There are, it would seem, missing scenes from 'Macbeth'. Improvise what happens in one of them;
   a Macduff entering the murder chamber (see II.iii.51);
   b Macbeth following him (see II.iii.51–72);
   c the execution of Cawdor (see I.iv);
   d discussion between Macbeth ('we will speak further', I.v.71) and Lady Macbeth ('what beast was't then', I.vii.47).

6 Dramatise a 'News at Ten' story on the incidents at Glamis Castle.

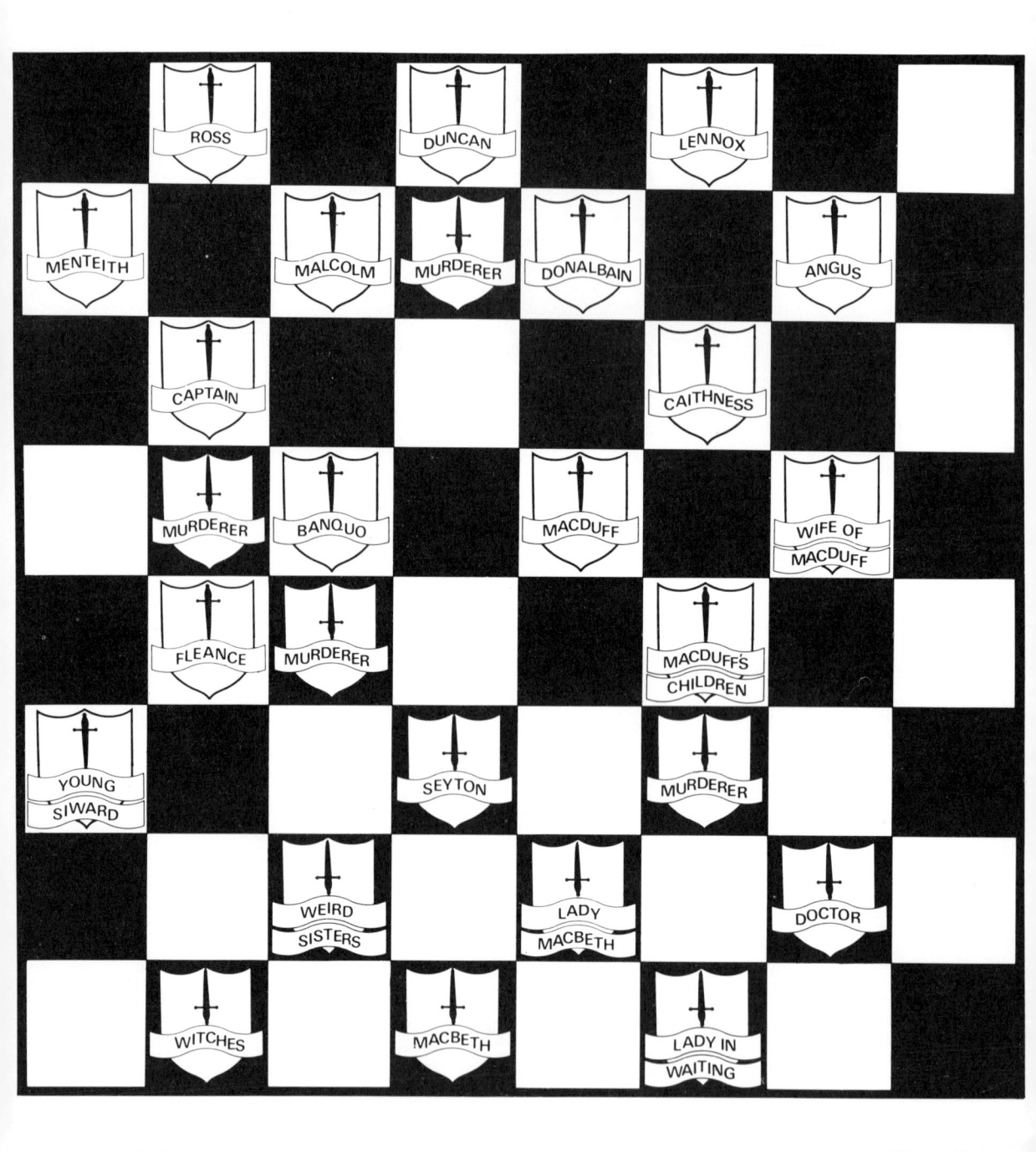

By looking at the 'chess board' showing the main characters of the play, you should easily be able to spot who is on whose side. Do you know who are the murdered people? If you are not sure, then look back at the story chart, find the 'murder' spots and then look them up in the text.

Although the 'chess board' names the characters, it does not tell us much about them. How can we find out more? This is not difficult if we use the 'People Pointers'.

'People Pointers'

– or what to look for to find out what a character is like.

This sounds difficult but is really easy – all you need to do is ask yourself how we form opinions about the people we meet in real life.

In making a decision about someone, some or all of the following factors are considered:
1. What do we learn of someone before we ever meet them?
2. What are the circumstances of their first appearance?
3. What are they wearing?
4. How do they look?
5. What do they say?
6. What do they think (if this can be found out)?
7. How do they act?
8. What do others say about them?
9. What do they say about others?
10. As we get to know them, how do they change?

These, then, are some questions which can help us to understand character. Some are more important than others. Now apply them to Macbeth. The answers should tell you which questions are most important.

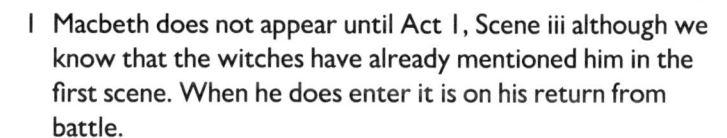

1. Macbeth does not appear until Act 1, Scene iii although we know that the witches have already mentioned him in the first scene. When he does enter it is on his return from battle.

2. He is immediately hailed by the three witches. The witches we know to be evil and it is here that they place the idea of the crown before Macbeth.
    'All hail, Macbeth, that shalt be king hereafter!' (I.iii)

    He is certainly interested because he tries to stop the witches before they vanish. Later, when he is given the title Thane (or Earl) of Cawdor, he says:
    **'Glamis, and Thane of Cawdor!
    The greatest is behind.'** (I.iii)

3. We do not know what Macbeth wears. However, as he is a soldier, and has just returned from battle, it is likely that he is in armour. We do know that at the end of the play, before the final battle, he asks for his armour.

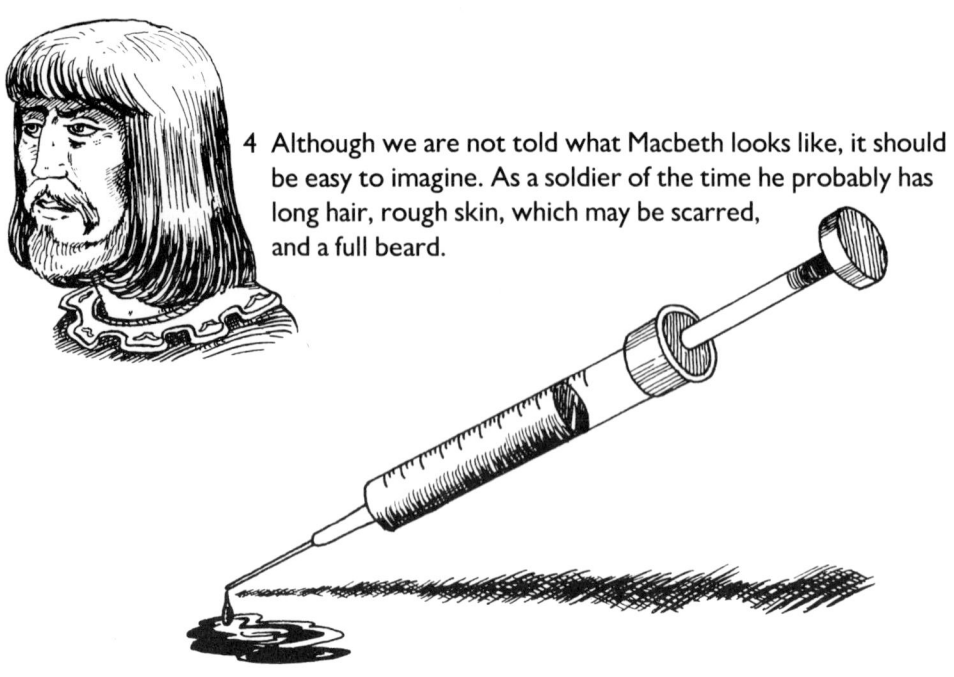

4 Although we are not told what Macbeth looks like, it should be easy to imagine. As a soldier of the time he probably has long hair, rough skin, which may be scarred, and a full beard.

'Out, damned spot! . . .'

5 By looking carefully through the play, it is possible to pick out some of the important things that Macbeth says:

**'If chance will have me king, why chance may crown me
   Without my stir.'** (I.iii)
**'Stars, hide your fires,
   Let not light see my black and deep desires.'** (I.iv)
**'If it were done when 'tis done, then 'twere well
   It were done quickly.'** (I.vii)
**'I have no spur
   to prick the sides of my intent but only
   Vaulting ambition . . .'** (I.vii)
**'Methought I heard a voice cry, "Sleep no more!
   Macbeth does murder sleep . . ."'** (II.ii)
**'I'll go no more.
   I am afraid to think what I have done;'** (II.ii)
'O, full of scorpions is my mind, dear wife!' (III.ii)

Even from these few quotations, many of which are said as 'asides', we can see the way Macbeth as a person begins to develop. He is impressed by the witches' prophecies but is prepared to wait on fate. Soon, however, his mind is occupied with what they have said. He has 'black and deep desires' which shortly are formed into a plan of action. After Duncan's murder he experiences terrible feelings of guilt. These are short-lived and quickly change to the 'scorpions' (deadly reptiles) of his mind which give him the power to do anything.

6   It is not possible to tell what someone is thinking because we cannot 'read' a mind. To show a person's thoughts Shakespeare uses what we call **soliloquy**, a moment when an actor, alone on the stage, says what he feels and what he is thinking.

Macbeth's soliloquy at the start of Act I, Scene vii shows his conscience at work. He realises that if he murders Duncan it will not be the end of the matter. He will destroy people's trust in him, and at the same time he will no longer be free to trust others. However, he is too consumed by ambition to forgo his plan.

In a similar way, Macbeth's soliloquy at the end of Act II, Scene i tells us what he is thinking immediately before he murders Duncan. Here the visionary dagger seems to float before him and lead him to the King's room. It is covered, both blade and handle, in drops of blood which suggest to Macbeth the idea of sacrifice. The ringing of the bell becomes in Macbeth's mind the death knell of Duncan.

7   Macbeth behaves in very different ways. With Duncan he is the strong soldier, loyal to his king. With the witches we see him consumed by evil, fascinated by their horrible beings. In private, with his wife, Lady Macbeth, he displays all of his secret hopes and fears, very often losing control of himself. On other occasions he is eaten up with ambition, cold and calculating, so that on learning of his wife's death he is able to say:
    'She should have died hereafter.' (V.v)

8   When we look at what other people say about Macbeth we see that different opinions are held. Duncan has nothing but praise for him and refers to him as 'noble Macbeth' (I.ii). This echoes the Captain's 'brave Macbeth – well he deserves that name' earlier in the same scene.

Banquo, Macbeth's close friend, at the start thinks of him as 'worthy' but later, after Duncan's murder, he suspects the truth:
    **'Thou hast it now: King, Cawdor, Glamis, all
    As the weird women promised; and I fear
    Thou playedst most foully for't.'** (III.i)

Lady Macbeth, the one person who really knows Macbeth, sees his weaknesses all too often:
    **'Yet I do fear thy nature:
    It is too full o' the milk of human-kindness
    To catch the nearest way.'** (I.v)

When his courage fails him, it is she who persuades him to go on:

> '**Wouldst thou have that**
> **Which thou esteem'st the ornament of life,**
> **And live a coward in thine own esteem,**
> **Letting "I dare not" wait upon "I would",**
> **Like the poor cat i' the adage?'** (I.vii)

and, when the deed is done and both are covered in blood, it is Lady Macbeth who sees her husband's terror:

> '**My hands are of your colour, but I shame**
> **To wear a heart so white.'** (II.ii)

9 It is perhaps most interesting to note what Macbeth says about Duncan, his first murder victim. Strangely he has enormous respect for him and feels that what he plots is wrong. This says something about Macbeth, doesn't it?

10 Macbeth certainly changes. From the man who fears to do evil at the start of the play, we watch the development of an almost separate person who becomes totally involved with evil and who lusts after position and power. It is sometimes difficult to realise that the man who is slain by Macduff is the one who is praised by Duncan.

Having made a fairly detailed study of Macbeth, let us describe him as simply as possible:

- M – urderous, menacing, . . .
- A – mbitious, . . .
- C – ourageous, . . .
- B – rutal, brave, . . .
- E – ager, . . .
- T – ormented, trusted, treacherous, . . .
- H – ated, . . .

Add to these qualities.

Now do the same for: Duncan,
Lady Macbeth,
Malcolm.

Can you do the same for Banquo?

Try to mime some of these descriptive words. See if others in your class can:
- a guess the character;
- b guess the mood.

Here are some more ideas to help you think about the characters:

1. What does Macbeth look like?
   Make and complete your own poster to find this dangerous man.

   # WANTED
   ## Dead or Alive
   ## 5,000 Sovereigns Reward

   ### MACBETH

   age _____   colour of eyes _____
   nationality _____   colour of hair _____
   crimes _____   hobbies _____

2. 'I dream't last night of the three Weird Sisters' (II.i). Describe Banquo's dream.

   Come, thick night ...

3   Before she dies, Lady Macbeth clearly goes mad (V.i). Today she would have been taken to a mental hospital where she could be treated properly and looked after. As her doctor you have to fill out her medical report form:

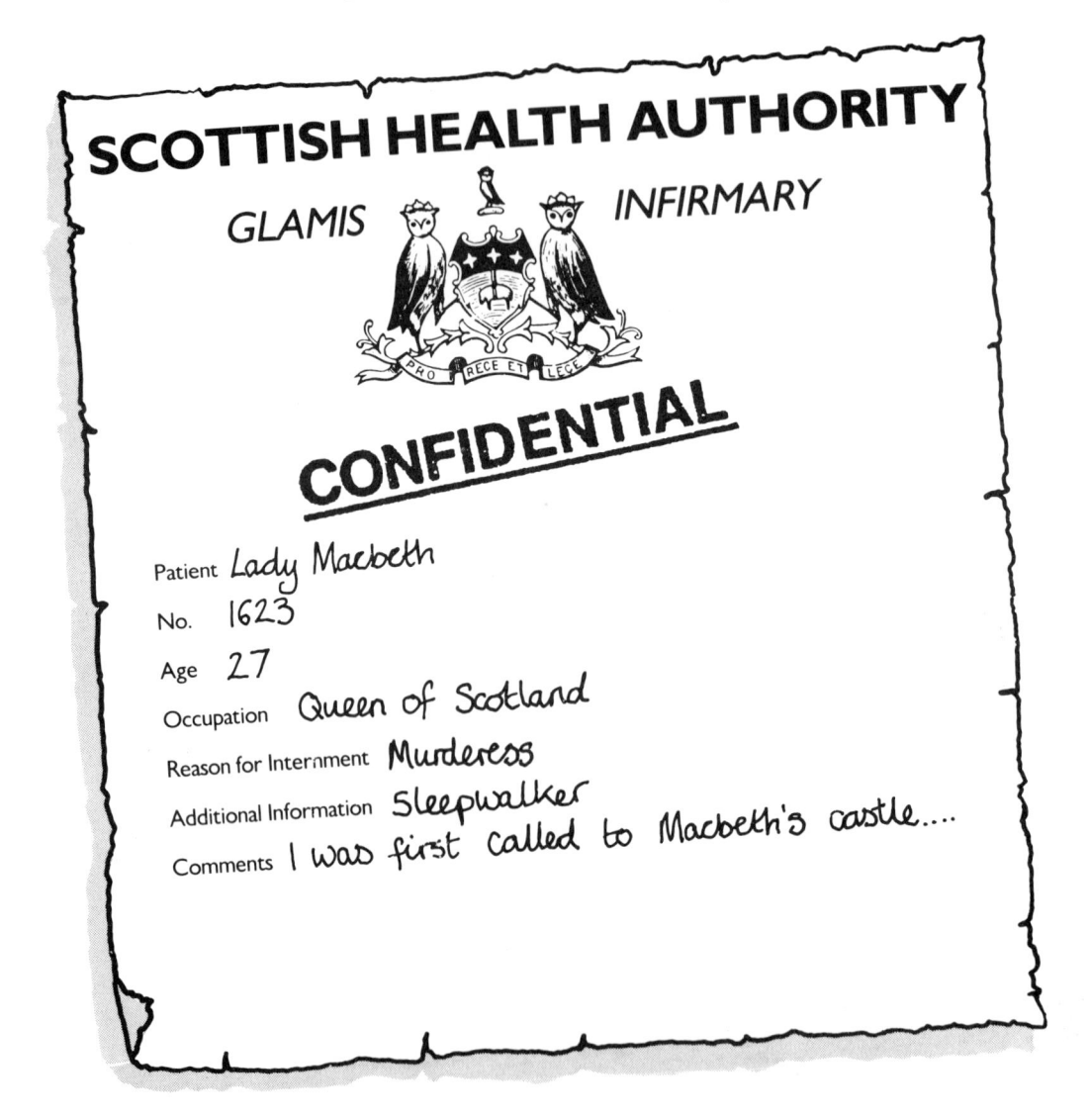

SCOTTISH HEALTH AUTHORITY

GLAMIS   *INFIRMARY*

CONFIDENTIAL

Patient *Lady Macbeth*
No. *1623*
Age *27*
Occupation *Queen of Scotland*
Reason for Internment *Murderess*
Additional Information *Sleepwalker*
Comments *I was first called to Macbeth's castle....*

4   'Come, you spirits
    That tend on mortal thoughts, unsex me here
    And fill me from the crown to the toe top-full
    Of direst cruelty.' (I.v)

   'I have given suck, and know
    How tender 'tis to love the babe that milks me;' (I.vii)

   Which of these quotations most accurately portrays the character of Lady Macbeth?

5 The Hag

The Hag is astride,
This night for to ride;
The Devill and shee together;
Through thick, and through thin,
Now out, and then in,
Though ne'r so foule be the weather.

A Thorn or a Burr
She takes for a Spurre:
With a lash of a Bramble she rides now,
Through Brakes and through Bryars,
O're Ditches, and Mires,
She followes the Spirit that guides now.

No Beast, for his food,
Dares now range the wood;
But husht in his laire he lies lurking;
While mischeifs, by these,
On Land and on Seas,
At noone of Night are a working.

The storme will arise,
And trouble the skies;
This night, and more for the wonder,
The ghost from the Tomb
Affrighted shall come,
Cal'd out by the clap of the Thunder.

ROBERT HERRICK

a Illustrate this poem.
b Describe some of the 'mischiefs' being worked.
c Write your own poem about the Witches in **Macbeth**.

6 To discover more about characters, try to imagine their behaviour in scenes not in the play. Improvise the characters in these situations:
   a Sweno, King of Norway, plotting rebellion with the Thane of Cawdor.
   b Lady Macbeth in conversation with Lady Banquo at Banquo's funeral.
   c Macduff exacting revenge on the captured murderers.
   d Reunion of Donalblain with Malcolm following Malcolm's coronation.
   e Fleance visiting the witches after Malcolm's coronation.

7 'This Is Your Life'. Improvise this programme with Macbeth as the celebrity. The supernatural is not ruled out, and strange guests from the past may appear!

8 'In the Psychiatrist's Chair'. Work in pairs. One is either Macbeth or Lady Macbeth, the other is the psychiatrist asking questions about their life. Tape some of these interviews and play them back to the whole group. A cross-examination by the group of some of the answers made will deepen understanding of the character.

9
   7   Elisha came to Damascus, at a time when Ben-hadad king
   8   of Aram was ill; and when he was told that the man of God had arrived, he bade Hazael take a gift with him and go to the man of God and inquire of the LORD through him
   9   whether he would recover from his illness. Hazael went, taking with him as a gift all kinds of wares of Damascus, forty camel-loads. When he came into the prophet's presence, he said, 'Your son Ben-hadad king of Aram has sent me to you to ask whether he will recover from his
   10 illness'. 'Go and tell him that he will recover', he
   11 answered; 'but the LORD has revealed to me that in fact he will die'. The man of God stood there with set face like a man stunned, until he could bear it no longer; then he
   12 wept. 'Why do you weep, my lord?' said Hazael. He answered, 'Because I know the harm you will do to the Israelites: you will set their fortresses on fire and put their young men to the sword; you will dash their children to
   13 the ground and you will rip open their pregnant women'. But Hazael said, 'But I am a dog, a mere nobody; how can I do this great thing?' Elisha answered, 'The LORD has revealed to me that you will be king of Aram'. Hazael left
   14 Elisha and returned to his master, who asked him what
   15 Elisha had said. 'He told me that you would recover', he replied. But the next day he took a blanket and, after dipping it in water, laid it over the king's face, and he died; and Hazael succeeded him.

(II Kings 8. 7–15)

Dramatise this story. Divide the action into various scenes. Supply additional characters. Provide dialogue.

Witches and Wishes

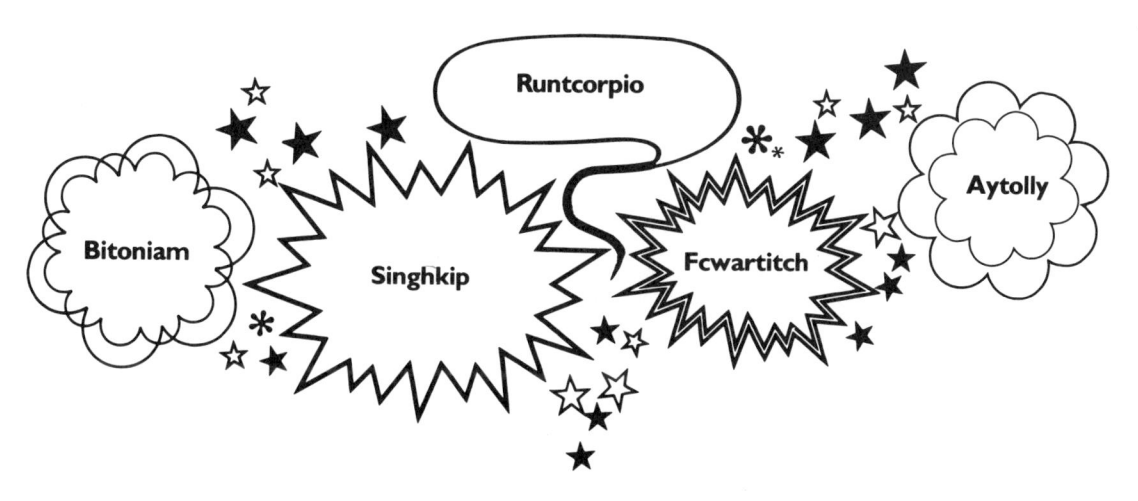

Bitoniam — *Singhkip* — *Runtcorpio* — *Fcwartitch* — *Aytolly*

> Double, double, toil and trouble,
> The words above are all a muddle!
> If you have a change-about
> All the themes come tumbling out!

You should by now have picked out the five main themes of the play. Perhaps there are others which you might have thought of, or would like to talk about with your teacher.

Obviously we cannot discuss all of these in detail. However, they are not all of equal importance but two, Witchcraft and Ambition, are central to the play.

Witchcraft

(I.i)   Notice how the witches are the first people we meet. Their 'evil' sets the scene of the play, whilst the thunder and lightning suggests the havoc that is to come. They are intent on meeting with Macbeth to tell him something they know will prey on his mind.

(I.iii)   In preparation for this meeting they cast their spells: 'Peace! The charm's wound up.' When Macbeth meets the witches he is fascinated by what they have to say. Banquo, on the other hand, puts the prophecy concerning himself out of his mind. Macbeth responds to the supernatural evil of the witches with an evil already in himself:

**'And oftentimes, to win us to our harm,
The instruments of darkness tell us truths.'**

(III.v) The witches, through their secret craft, already know that Macbeth will come to seek them out.

**'Thither he
Will come, to know his destiny.'**

Accordingly, they prepare.

(IV.i) In a cavern, against a background of thunder, the three witches cast their spells to summon spirits who will answer Macbeth's questions. Interestingly, even the witches acknowledge Macbeth's evil nature:

**'By the pricking of my thumbs,
Something wicked this way comes.'**

Macbeth's first meeting with the witches was 'accidental', his second is deliberate. Now, totally immersed in the forces of darkness, he demands to 'see' the future. They respond and present him with a series of four pictures ('apparitions').

1 An armed head.
2 A bloody child.
3 A child crowned with a tree in his hand.
4 A show of eight kings, followed by Banquo's ghost.

What do these four pictures mean? Macbeth knows, takes comfort from the first three but is upset by the last. The witches dance and vanish.

From this we can see how the supernatural is used in the play to:
1. **expose** the evil hiding in Macbeth;
2. **direct** his evil to particular deeds;
3. **highlight** the forces of evil at work in the world;
4. **create** atmosphere in the play.

Of course, the witches' spells in Act IV.i can be seen in a lighter vein. Have you ever thought of them as a recipe? Pick out and make a list of all the ingredients (perhaps draw them as well). You may even like to put them into a rhyme of your own as we have done.

This baboon's blood
Makes such bad food!
And blind worm's sting –
A nasty thing.
And hemlock root
Helps vomit sprout.
And as for snake –
It gives gut ache.

You will see that, like Shakespeare, we have written in rhyme. This helps to create a sense of magic. Does your spell rhyme?

Some Spooky Suggestionsssss

1. Make a tape recording of Act IV.i. Try to create an exciting atmosphere by sound effects and different voices for the parts. Find yourself some eerie music to go with it.

2. How 'it' strikes a cat. Grey-Malkin has seen some very strange goings-on. Now she reveals all. What does she say?

3. Runes are the secret letters of witches. Make up your own magic code and then write a secret message to your friend.
    33913   our code !!!

4. Write an advertisement for a witch's potion.

5. Draw a cartoon strip for each of the four apparitions which appear before Macbeth.

6. Read the story of the Witch of Endor, I. Samuel, 28. How is this different from Macbeth's meeting?

7 # Sonnet 72

    Hallowe'en. She dressed up in a sheet,
A paper crown, a tail, a fierce expression,
High-button shoes, not fitting, on her feet,
A broken mask, her proudest child-possession,
A lantern on the handle of a broom,
While over the sky of her anticipation,
Shining and far away though in that room
Feet, lantern, hands leapt like a constellation.
Outdoors she waved her lantern in wild daring
And yelled at a stranger passing in the night,
Half to cheer herself and half in play.
But scared herself with her own sudden scaring,
And ran from what she thought would run away,
And found she could not even frighten fright.

PAUL ENGLE

Hallowe'en is the night of the year for witches.

Why is it called Hallowe'en?

What used to happen on this night?

How is it celebrated today?

Find out all you can.

8 **Either** complete this story:

    Only the change in the level of the ground at his feet told him when he at last came to the top of a ridge or hill. He was weary, sweating and yet chilled. It was wholly dark.
    'Where are you?' he cried out miserably.
    There was no reply. He stood listening. He was suddenly aware that it was getting very cold, and that up here a wind was beginning to blow, an icy wind.

J. R. TOLKEIN: **The Lord of The Rings**

Or write your own story to end in this way:

    This was the pass, and the end. There was no way further. The end of the level ground was the edge of a cliff: beyond it the darkness went on forever, and the small stars hung unmoving in the black gulf of the sky.
    Endurance may outlast hope. He crawled forward, when he was able to do so, doggedly. He looked over the edge of darkness. And below him, only a little way below, he saw the beach of ivory sand; and white and amber waves were curling and breaking foam on it, and across the sea the sun setting in a haze of gold.

URSULA LEGUIN: **The Earthsea Trilogy**

9   Two people visit a fortune teller and are told they are going to be exceedingly rich. One ignores the prediction, the other helps it along. In groups, devise the two dramatic sketches which show the fortune or otherwise of the two people.

10 The ghost of Banquo upsets Macbeth's banquet. Improvise a party scene where everything is going wonderfully well, until the arrival of an unexpected visitor.

Ambition

Macbeth's ambition is to be King of Scotland; he will be King of Scotland – by fair means or foul. As soon as the witches declare the prophecy (I.iii), Banquo notices that Macbeth is 'rapt withal' – withdrawn in contemplating his 'royal hope'.

Later on in the same act we find in Macbeth's asides his real view of the 'royal hope' set before him. Even as the title of Cawdor is bestowed upon him, it becomes empty of significance because 'the greatest is behind'. Macbeth's sights are not on Glamis or Cawdor, but on the kingship which follows behind them.

Glamis and Cawdor are simply 'happy prologues' – mere introductions – compared with the matter of genuine importance:

> **the swelling Act**
> **Of the imperial theme.** (I.iii)

Already Macbeth is considering murder in order to obtain the crown. His ambition is relentlessly driving him on.

However, there is a conflict between his ambition and his conscience. Lady Macbeth sees this (I.v). Her own ambition is that her husband should be king. Therefore, she works to remove his doubts.

So, supported by his wife, Macbeth's 'vaulting ambition' (I.vii) enables him to leap over all obstacles which prevent his becoming king. But once king, Macbeth's ambition is not satisfied. He must remain king. He must crush all opposition. He staggers from one bloody murder to another to ensure his and his family's hold upon the crown.

The more Macbeth murders, the more the opposition against him hardens. In particular, the brutal killing of Lady Macduff and her children (IV.ii) turns Macduff – the one man Macbeth needs to fear (IV.i) – into a deadly enemy (IV.iii). Macbeth's ambitions to be king, and for his children to succeed him, are defeated when he faces Macduff on the battlefield (V.vi).

Ambition Additions

1 Here is Macbeth climbing his ladder of ambition.

    a What are the rungs on your ladder? Draw it and label the rungs.
    b Is the ladder of ambition endless? Is it for Macbeth? Is it for you?
    c Do we ever deliberately climb down the ladder?
    d Does everyone have ambition?
    e What is meant by 'failed ambition'? Can it be a good thing?
    f 'The higher we climb, the further we fall'. Is this an accurate view of ambition?

2 Macbeth is dead. Ambition like his lives on. Find out about people, past or present, who have been fired with ambition.

3 You are made king. You publish a 'Royal Proclamation' setting out your wishes. Present this work in the form of a scroll.

4 Macbeth has a guilty conscience, a result of the murders and misdeeds he has committed. Write about a time when you had feelings of guilt because of something you had done.

Like a King...

Lady Macbeth says to Macbeth:
> **'The sleeping and the dead
> Are but as pictures'** (II.ii)

in order to calm his fears. He needs to have his fears calmed: he has just murdered Duncan, the King. Suppose he is discovered and then ... justice would take its course, and that would be something to be afraid of. But it is not that kind of fear that is obsessing Macbeth, or that Lady Macbeth is trying to calm. Macbeth's fear is far deeper.

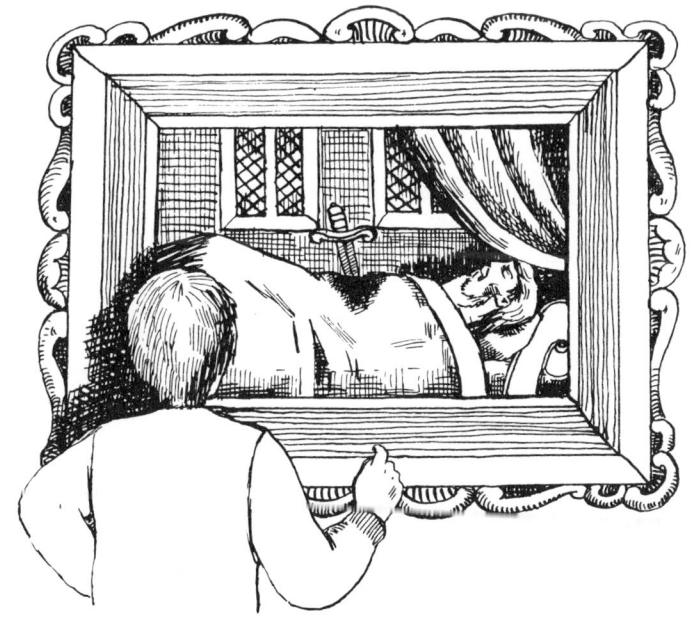

On returning from the murder chamber Macbeth hears, or thinks he hears, a voice crying:
> **'Sleep no more! Macbeth does murder sleep'.**

Is this a supernatural voice haunting him, or is it his guilty conscience condemning him? Macbeth finds he can no longer say 'Amen'. The full horror of the deed strikes his mind so that he is:
> **'afraid to think what I have done'.**

He has left Duncan dead, and Duncan's two sons sleeping – could the dead or the sleeping cry out?

Lady Macbeth seeks to reassure Macbeth that the sleeping and the dead cannot cry out, that Macbeth's fears are irrational – there are no devils, ghosts or ghouls to fear – so she says:

**'The sleeping and the dead
Are but as pictures.'**

In other words, they are **like** pictures. They share certain qualities in common with pictures.

When we say something is 'like' or 'as' something else, we are using a **simile**.

In what ways are the sleeping and the dead like a picture? List all the possible similarities. Your list will include:

Sleeping and dead people:
- immobile
- static
- unchanging
- lifeless
- arouse the imagination
- are seen, but cannot see
- are silent

Consider the following similes from **Macbeth**, and list the similarities as we have done above.

1. The wolf moves **like a ghost**.
2. A heavy summons lies **like lead upon me**.
3. Black Macbeth will seem **as pure as snow**.
4. Esteem him **as a lamb**.
5. Now does he feel his title hang loose about him, **like a giant's robe upon a dwarfish thief**.

When you have done this, complete these similes. We have done the first two for you:

Macbeth's anger was **like a volcano erupting**.
Macbeth seemed as deadly **as a scorpion**.
Duncan was like . . .
The witches were as wicked as . . .
Banquo's nobility was like . . .
Lady Macbeth's love for Macbeth was like . . .
Macbeth's brightly polished sword shone as . . .
Lady Macbeth's well washed hands looked like . . .
Lady Macduff seemed like . . . when she faced her murderers.
Murderers are much the same as . . .

You should now be able to make up your own similes. Try to make them as lively and imaginative as possible. Why not also see how many others you are able to find in the play?

... A King Uprooted

Duncan says to Macbeth:
> **'Welcome hither.**
> **I have begun to plant thee, and will labour**
> **To make thee full of growing.'** (I.iv)

What strange things to say! Can you see what Duncan means?

He cannot mean he is going to plant Macbeth literally, can he? Of course not! We need to look at what has happened to understand what Duncan means.
1. Macbeth has destroyed the king's deadly enemies.
2. The king is grateful and has already rewarded Macbeth by granting him the title Thane of Cawdor.
3. Duncan wants to give Macbeth a greater reward.

This helps us to see the meaning of 'plant'. The king views Macbeth as a plant which he looks after by rewarding with favours. The more favours he grants, the more Macbeth 'grows'.

> When we use a word in a non-literal sense, we say we use it **metaphorically**. So 'plant' in this sense is a **metaphor**.

33

Here are some examples:

Literal	Metaphorical
Lady Macbeth waters seeds in her garden.	Lady Macbeth waters the seeds of murder in Macbeth's mind.

Now, with the sentences below, put them into their proper column. Are they literal or metaphorical?

    Who can bid the tree unfix his earth-bound root?
    But myself should be the root and father of many kings.
    Upon my head they placed a fruitless crown.
    I will advise you where to plant yourselves.
    Macbeth's actions bear no good fruit, but merely the leaves of bitterness.
    The lemon plant has a delicious smell, but its leaves are bitter.
    The witches often used leaves, twigs, and small branches in their magical spells.
    Macbeth's ambition flowered.

All our examples so far have been taken from gardening. This need not be the case:
    'Come, seeling night,
Scarf up the tender eye of pitiful day.' (III.iii)
    '... yet know not what we fear,
But float upon a wild and violent sea.' (IV.ii)
    'Out, out, brief candle!
Life's but a walking shadow, ...' (V.v)

Make up your own metaphors about the following. We have done the first one for you in three different ways.

1. Darkness ... **is a blanket on the day.**
              strangles the body of light.
              seals the cracks of hope.
2. Macbeth's crown ...
3. Macbeth's castle ...
4. Murder ...
5. Fear ...
6. Treason ...
7. Loyalty ...
8. Ambition ...
9. Witchcraft ...
10. Marriage ...

Stages of the Story

The stage

Story, people, ideas, words are all ingredients in **Macbeth**. But **Macbeth** is also a play to be performed on a stage. And a stage is that area where action takes place.

At different times there have been different types of stage. In Shakespeare's day the stage looked like this:

This is called a **thrust stage**. You will see that:
1. it is raised;
2. it is built out 'into' the audience;
3. it is partly covered.

Today a thrust stage might look like this:

Notice that now it is no longer covered – the theatre itself has a roof!

The advantages of a thrust stage are:
 1 it brings the players close to the audience;
 2 it gives the players considerable freedom of movement;
 3 it reduces the need for a background.

Imagine the effect of these advantages in **Macbeth**. For example:

1 V.i.   Lady Macbeth is sleepwalking. It is night. It is dark. A small candle burns. She is guilty. She is mad. She rubs her hands ... blood? ... she advances towards YOU, the audience ... down the long thrust stage. Somewhere in the background you hear the voices of a doctor and lady-in-waiting describing her awful condition. She draws near.

2 II.iii.   Duncan has been murdered – 'Confusion now hath made his masterpiece.' All the major characters tumble onto the stage: Macbeth, Macduff, Malcolm, Donalbain, Lady Macbeth and Banquo. Disorder – Macduff is grief-stricken, Macbeth pretends outrage, Lady Macbeth faints, Malcolm and Donalbain plan escape, and Banquo attempts to bring control back.

3 I.iii.   Three witches prepare themselves for a meeting with Macbeth and Banquo. No background of painted scenery required: positioning, movement, lighting and voice create the atmosphere of evil. The size of the thrust stage allows for plenty of room to experiment. Just how surprised can Banquo be when he says, 'What are these ...?' Do the witches appear in front, from behind, around, or encircled by Macbeth and Banquo?

From desks or rostra blocks make your own thrust stage.

Now tackle these three scenes. Discover for yourself the three advantages of a thrust stage.
 1 I.iv.   The King's Court
 2 III.iv. The Banquet
 3 V.iv & vi.   The Army: Birnam Wood advancing on Dunsinane.

Costume, Sound and Effects

Costume

The clothes the players wear are called **costumes**. Careful choice of colours + designs + textures = the best effect

Look at the pictures below:

In each case the costume 'adds' to the character. Which two pictures do you think are of Macbeth? Why are the other two unsuitable?

Ian McKellen is dressed in black to play Macbeth. Black is used to suggest darkness, secrecy, and evil.

On the other hand, Paul Schofield is in white. Can you think of reasons for this? One possible answer may be found in I.v.63–64.

Certain other colours may be used in similar ways – red and purple for royalty, green for envy. Can you think of more?

Elizabethan dress tended to be very full and rich in appearance. Because of this it is difficult (and expensive) to copy effectively. Too much detail may appear fussy and may not show up on the stage. The most rewarding designs are often the simplest.

Texture
In costume design the texture of the material is important. Coarse soft fabrics tend to absorb light and give an appearance of depth and solidity. The opposite effect is gained with materials which reflect light.

Design costumes for these characters for your own **Macbeth** production:
- Duncan I.vi.
- Porter II.iii.
- Murderer III.iii.
- Lady Macbeth III.iv.
- Macbeth III.iv.
- Three Witches IV.i.

You may also like to think about how Macbeth and Lady Macbeth will be dressed in other scenes.

Choose any scene(s) from the play which you feel could be played in modern dress. Give reasons for your choice(s).

Select one item of costume. Build a character around it. Develop the character into a mime. Once you have done this, involve two or more other 'characters'.

Sound

Music and sound are important in most plays. This is because they help to create atmosphere. The kind of music chosen will match the atmosphere. Is the scene jolly, sad, tense, foreboding, fantastic, destructive, tender, brutal, reconciliatory?

It must be remembered that silence itself can be a form of music. What atmosphere could silence evoke?

If we look at **Macbeth** we see that there are plenty of directions for music and sound.

In Act I we find the stage directions:
- I.i. Thunder
- I.ii. Alarum within
- I.iii. Thunder
- I.iii.28 Drum within
- I.iv. Flourish
- I.iv.59 Flourish
- I.vi. Hautboys* and torches   * hautboys = oboes
- I.vii. Hautboys

These sounds and musical directions set the mood of the scenes:
- thunder suggests awe and mystery;
- alarum suggests war and disorder;
- flourish suggests triumph and dignity.

Now go through the play and write down any other musical/sound directions, noting the scene in which they occur.

The scene which uses most music and sound is IV.i. Discuss the atmosphere of this scene and how sound and music could contribute.

What music would you use for:
- IV.i.44   Music and a song: 'Black Spirits'
- IV.i.104 Hautboys
- IV.i.131 Music. The Witches dance; and vanish?

This scene also offers an opportunity for choral work. Break into groups of a dozen or so, allow individuals to read out 1st, 2nd and 3rd Witch, but experiment with larger numbers chanting the 'All' parts. Try the passages several times, vary the speed of the reading. What pace is the most effective? And why?

Often before plays even begin music is played to the audience. This helps to put the audience in the right frame of mind. What frame of mind would suit **Macbeth**? Discuss musical ideas for this, and arrange a session for everyone to bring his or her choice of music in, and to play it.

Stage props

As well as costume, most plays will make use of stage properties (props). A stage prop is an article or item of furniture used by the players.

Nowadays most theatre companies have a large selection of props. In Shakespeare's time props were fewer and simpler. A list might include: a crown, a rock, a golden sceptre, a bay tree, a coffin.

Look at I.iv. and V.i. and decide what props are necessary.

Players

A theatre production depends most of all upon the players.

It is possible to imagine no director, no designers, and even no proper stage – but whenever a player goes before an audience, then there is theatre.

The players' job is to make the audience **suspend disbelief**. The audience knows that what it is seeing is not **really** happening. But when the acting is convincing, the audience is prepared to believe in the reality of the action.

Of course, there is **never** only one way to play a part. Theatre constantly gives us a fresh approach to a familiar role.

Sarah Siddons 200 hundred years ago, Ellen Terry 100 years ago, and Judi Dench more recently, have all been Lady Macbeth.

Sarah Siddons by Gainsborough (1755–1831)   Ellen Terry by John Sargent (1847–1928)

'Some actresses ... aimed at a very different response. Mrs Siddons made Lady Macbeth human, and gave her "the graces of personal beauty", while Ellen Terry's performance was "pungent with the **odeur de femme** ... she rushed into her husband's arms, clinging, kissing, coaxing, flattering".'

Judi Dench (1934–)

Judi Dench said, when she came to play the role:

Lady Macbeth is first and foremost a woman, with a woman's weaknesses and instincts. Her ambition is not for herself but for her husband. There is such a tremendous physical passion between them that she feels he only deserves the best. All they have to achieve is one act, that of murdering Duncan. That is why she calls upon the spirits – to make her strong, to stop her from being weak and womanly, and thus she gains amazing power.

She doesn't, however, bargain for the rift that occurs between her and Macbeth after the murder. She thinks she has attained his goal but once he has tasted blood he cannot stop. When he asks to be alone she sees a crack for the first time and she was not prepared for isolation. At the banquet she requires supernatural endurance and afterwards she is drained of everything. There is nothing left.

She is last seen in her sleep-walking state when through guilt and sleepless torment she has been pushed to the edge of sanity.

Her final cry is a death rattle. She who was once so strong for her husband, when deprived of his support, is just a shell.

JUDI DENCH

These comments show how a player attempts to understand and seeks to identify with a character. It is this process that leads to a convincing performance.

Try it yourself. In I.v. Lady Macbeth enters. She is composed and reading her husband's letter. How does the mood change when:
- she has read the letter (I.v.13)?
- the messenger leaves (I.v.36)?
- Macbeth enters (I.v.52)?
- she learns Duncan proposes to leave (I.v.58)?

Act out this scene. Pay attention to movement, gesture, facial expression, voice. These should indicate the different moods of the characters in the scene.

The three pictures show women playing the part of Lady Macbeth. There are no pictures of women playing the part in Elizabethan times. This is because women were not allowed to perform on stage. Female roles were played by young boys.

The director

In staging any play many decisions have to be taken. The final decision maker in the theatre is the **director**.

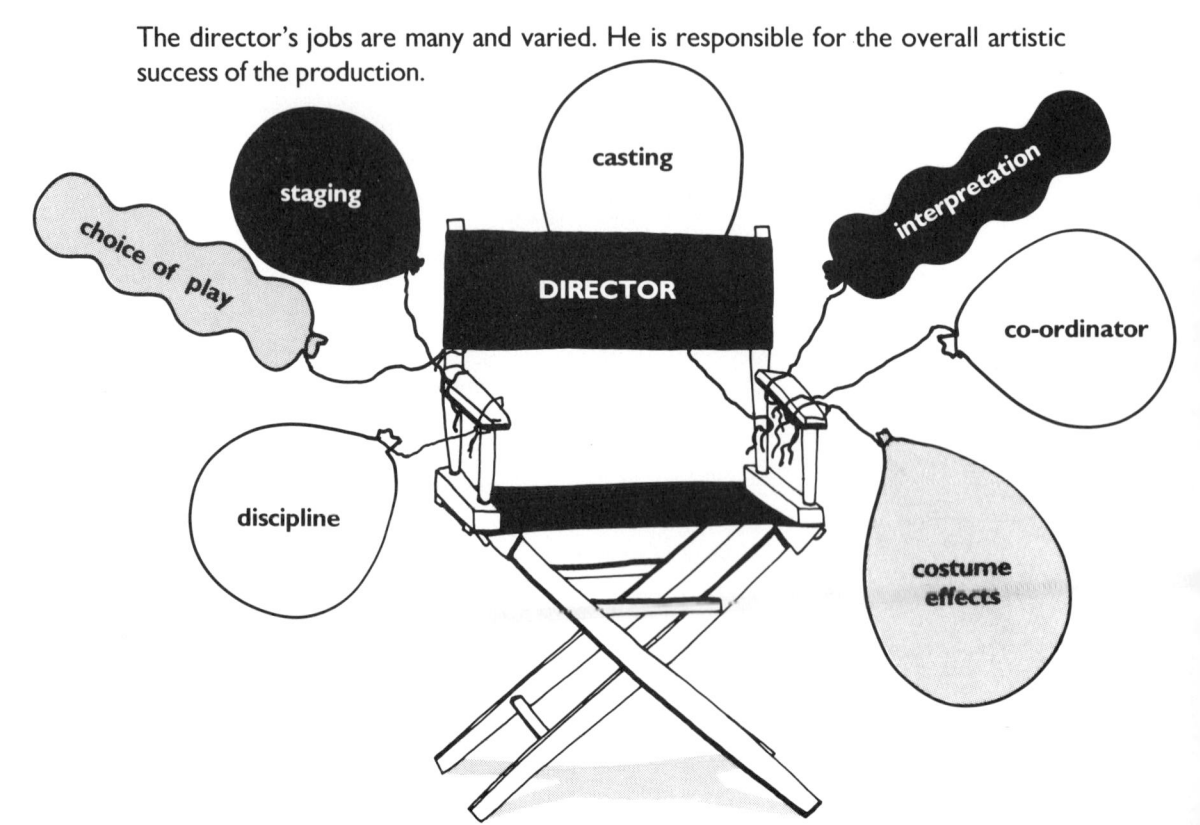

The director's jobs are many and varied. He is responsible for the overall artistic success of the production.

- choice of play
- staging
- casting
- interpretation
- co-ordinator
- costume effects
- discipline

DIRECTOR

Look at the opening scene of **Macbeth**.

Thunder and lightning. Enter three Witches   1.1

FIRST WITCH
   When shall we three meet again?
   In thunder, lightning, or in rain?
SECOND WITCH
   When the hurly-burly's done,
   When the battle's lost and won.
THIRD WITCH
   That will be ere the set of sun.
FIRST WITCH
   Where the place?
SECOND WITCH Upon the heath.
THIRD WITCH
   There to meet with Macbeth.
FIRST WITCH
   I come, Grey-Malkin.
SECOND WITCH   Paddock calls!
THIRD WITCH   Anon!
ALL
   Fair is foul, and foul is fair.
   Hover through the fog and filthy air.   **Exeunt**

The stage directions, '**Thunder and lightning. Enter three Witches**', do not tell us much. There are all kinds of questions we could ask:
   How fierce is the storm?
   From where do the witches appear?
   Are they together?
   How are they dressed?
Nor, when we read the lines, is it clear how they are to be said. This is something else to decide.

It is the job of the director to ask questions about the play, then to answer them. How he answers them will show how he interprets the play – what meanings he wishes to explain, which themes he intends to bring out. To sort out all the different questions to be asked, he could put them under headings:

?

character
relationships
gesture/expression
movement
costume/set
music/sound/lighting

So, under the heading of COSTUME/SET he will consider the witches' clothing, its colour, texture, style, and the way in which the stage is to look for the opening scene. How evil the witches are will depend upon the ideas the director has about their characters.

In groups, discuss questions that could be asked about this scene. Arrange the questions under the suggested headings.

The director will not simply tell the cast what to do in every detail. He will be just as interested in hearing their ideas. In his director's notes, Trevor Nunn has this to say about his production of **Macbeth**:

> 'If Shakespeare writes a play about something he will always include a play about its opposite. So in **Macbeth** when he writes a play that concerns itself with faith, it also becomes a play about the absence of faith.'
>
> * * * * *
>
> '... then, for the first time, I decided to chalk out a circle on the floor; the play would be performed within that circular area.'
>
> * * * * *
>
> 'I had extremely inventive leading actors who were convinced of the thinking that had already been brought to bear upon the play.'

The final interpretation will be the result of much discussion and improvisation. Because of this, a single, innocent line may be filled with emotion merely by a look, gesture, slight movement, or even a silence.

Read the following lines:

>   MACBETH: If chance will have me King, why chance may crown me
>   Without my stir. (I.iii)
>   MACBETH: I have done the deed. Didst thou hear a noise? (II.ii)
>   LADY MACBETH: What's the business,
>   That such a hideous trumpet calls to parley
>   The sleepers of the house? Speak, speak! (II.iii)
>   FIRST MURDERER: Most royal sir – Fleance is scaped. (III.iv)
>   ROSS: Your castle is surprised, your wife and babes
>   Savagely slaughtered. (IV.iii)
>   SEYTON: The queen, my lord, is dead. (V.v)

Study what happens before and after them. Decide how you think these lines may best be said. Can you give reasons for your decisions?

Group work: choose either III.iii or IV.ii. Discuss how the scene is to be presented. Practise improvisation. Act it out to the rest of the class.

Facial expressions, gesture and movement are all important. The director must see that they are appropriate. Working in pairs, one as director, one as player, show:
1. Lady Macbeth reading her husband's letter (I.v).
2. The joy of Duncan arriving at Glamis Castle (I.vi).
3. Macbeth recoiling from Banquo's ghost (III.iv).
4. The amazement of the Doctor watching Lady Macbeth (V.i).
5. The triumph of Macduff displaying Macbeth's head (V.vi).

P.S. Macbeth is traditionally a very, very unlucky play.

'As well as being a huge technical challenge to actors and directors, **Macbeth** has the added disadvantage, in a notoriously superstitious profession, of being considered unlucky. Actors regale one another with tales of broken limbs and other disasters incurred while performing in it, and there is a tradition that one doesn't even mention it by name: it is referred to as 'the Scottish play'.

Sybil Thorndike's account of how she and her husband Lewis Casson warded-off trouble from a production in which they were jointly involved confirms this superstition.

Dreadful things kept recurring, reaching such frightful proportions that Lewis called me into his room and said, 'Sybil, the devil does work in this play. There is horror behind it. We must do something positive against it.' And together we read aloud the Ninety-first Psalm, which quieted and strengthened us and made us feel normal again.'

DIANA RIGG

Criticism

It may come as a surprise, but we are all critics! Often when we hear a record, or watch television, we give an opinion. We may say the music is wonderful, or the programme is terrible. Usually someone then says, 'Why? Why is it wonderful? Why is it terrible?' As soon as we give reasons, we are **criticising**. And we are becoming **critics.**

It is important to realise that criticism is not just fault-finding. Critics praise as well as blame.

Every member of a theatre audience can be critical, but often professional critics are present too. The professional critic is paid to criticise. That is their job. They write a report about what they have seen. They tell the public, 'See this . . . it is good because . . .' **or** 'Avoid that . . . it is bad because . . .'

It is all a matter of opinion – opinions backed up with reasons and arguments.

What reasons count for the critics? And what arguments do they use?

> 'I confess that I never thought to see the speech beginning 'What beast was't then that made you break this enterprise to me?' with the speaker reclining in abandonment and luxury in the arms of her sheikh on an art-coloured divan with a distant gramophone playing the opening of the first act of Carmen.'
> JAMES AGATE

- lack of tension?
- set unsuitable?
- thematically wrong music?

> 'He would make a sinister Shylock, a frightening Fagin. But this Thane of Cawdor would be unnerved by Banquo's valet, never mind Banquo's ghost . . .'
> ALAN BRIEN

- miscasting?
- correct interpretation of character?

> 'He strides on in what one first takes to be the last stages of battle fatigue. His walk is an exhausted lunge, his voice thick, hoarse and full of abrupt sledgehammer emphases. But as he begins, so he continues. His manner on the stage is not that of a man in an intricate, danger-fraught situation, but that of someone who owns the place.'
> IRVING WARDLE

- appropriate posture?
- suitable movement?
- misreading of character and situation?
- lack of development?
- is this overdramatic?

pace measured?

'On the battlements Sir Laurence's throttled fury (switches) into top gear, and we see a lion, baffled but still colossal. "I 'gin to be a-weary of the sun" held the very ecstasy of despair, the actor swaying with grief, his voice rising like hair on the crest of a trapped animal.'

KENNETH TYNAN

interpretation right?

movement and voice effective?

small parts convincing?

'Besides delivering their speeches with vigorous authenticity, thanes and hired assassins alike bring plenty of convincing toughness to the play's physical struggles. There is, too, a nicely inventive treatment of the bearing of Birnam Wood to Dunsinane: spring-like green light just flickers over the army supposedly carrying branches, giving an effect of freshly sprouting life.'

PETER KEMP

play's requirements met?

lighting develops play's theme?

Now read the following review. Certain words have been underlined. What critical points can be made?

Visually, Gold works tactfully and powerfully to highlight the pervading imagery. Blood spouts and cakes effectively. Mist and darkness thicken an atmosphere of uncertainty and evil. The sets have the slab-like simplicity of the play's structure: Dunsinane is a chunky assemblage of grim walls, forbidding corridors and few loopholes; the witches convene near a cromlech – and, when crouched motionless in their grey rags, look like eerie prehistoric boulders.

Banquo's ghost never materialises: Macbeth does indeed, as the camera emphasises, look but on a stool. The apparitions in Act Four don't appear either. Instead, the production has Macbeth inhaling narcotic fumes from the hags' cauldron and staring, mesmerised, into it, as the witches ventriloquise spirit voices.

Apparently seeing Macbeth as schizophrenic, Nicol Williamson employs two different vocal registers for him – a ringing, resonant tone for public utterance, and a hoarse, introverted mutter for private disturbance. Increasingly exaggerated, this split-level approach eventually breaks up the character, as well as the sense of numerous lines. In particular, Macbeth's final scenes – all ogreish howls and rapid simian gibber – are drastically reduced to sound and fury, signifying nothing.

With the casting of Jane Lapotaire as Lady Macbeth, further damage is done. An actress who – in voice, looks and technique – is most suited to mannered comedy, she gives a fatally lightweight performance. The 'fiendlike queen' becomes a girlish figure crooning 'My husband!' in tones that would do credit to a Barbara Cartland heroine.

Only in the sleep-walking scene does she turn her ingenuity to bringing out what's in the play instead of superimposing things alien to it: in a neatly chilling touch, she uses the conventional outstretched-arms posture of the sleep-walker to portray Lady Macbeth pushing her rigid, tainted hands as far from her as possible.

PETER KEMP **Times Literary Supplement** (18.11.1983)